CW00473422

Real Grappling

Geoff Thompson

SUMMERSDALE

First published 1994.

This edition copyright © Geoff Thompson 1998

Reprinted 2000

All rights reserved.

No part of this book may be reproduced by any means, nor transmitted, nor translated into a machine language, without the written permission of the publisher.

Summersdale Publishers Ltd
46 West Street
Chichester
West Sussex
PO19 1RP
United Kingdom

www.summersdale.com

Printed and bound in Great Britain.

ISBN 1 84024 086 5

Please note: the author and the publishers cannot accept any responsibility for any prosecutions or proceedings brought or instituted against any person or body as a result of the use or misuse of any techniques described in this book or any loss, injury or damage caused thereby.

About the Author:

Geoff Thompson has to be one of the most recognised and controversial martial arts writers and teachers of this century, with over 20 best-selling books and 20 instructional videos on the contemporary role of martial art to his name. His work is both innovative and thought-provoking. As an ambassador for the martial arts he has appeared on national and international television and radio – for several years as the *BBC Good Morning* self-defence expert – talking about and giving advice on self-protection and related subjects.

He has taught his unique method of self-protection to the police, the Royal Marine commandos, in local government, on Excel Bodyguard training camps and also on the professional circuit. Geoff's first book *Watch My Back – A Bouncer's Story* (released in the USA by Paladin Press) about his nine years working as a nightclub doorman is widely recognised as a cult book. His other books have also been highly successful. He has appeared in numerous publications including: *SG's Martial Arts*, *Combat*, *Traditional Karate*, *Fighters*, *Terry O'Neill's Fighting Arts International*, *Muscle Mag* (Britain – USA), *Black Belt Magazine* (USA) *Fighters* (Sweden) and *Australasian Fighting Arts* (Australia). He is currently Sub-Editor of *Martial Arts Illustrated*. He has also featured in mainstream glossy magazines such as *Loaded*, *Maxim* and *Esquire* and has published several articles with *GQ* Magazine (Britain – Paris).

Geoff has to be one of the most practised instructors of our day with a long list of combat qualifications. He is presently a Sambo Russian Wrestling coach (Moscow Sambo Federation), Olympic Greco Roman Wrestling Coach (FILA), Olympic Free Style Level 3 Wrestling Coach (FILA) Ju-Jitsu coach, British Combat Association Coach, EKGB (Karate) 5th Dan, JKA (Japan Karate

Association) 2nd Dan, Shoalin Modga gung fu 1st Dan, BJA (British Judo Association) 1st Dan, ABA boxing coach and BTBC Muay Thai boxing coach. He is a former UK weapons champion and is trained in the use of the Defensive Flashlight and the PR24 Side Handled Baton. He has also trained in Aikido and weapons.

In 1997 Geoff was flown out to the United States by Chuck Norris and Richard Norton to teach his unique method of self-protection on their international martial arts seminar alongside martial art greats: Benny 'the jet' Urquediz and Rigan and Jean-Jacques Machado.

As well as his books and videos Geoff has written a feature film based on his life and 12 television plays based on his bouncer books. Although recognised as an international authority on the art of self-protection, his work in reality and cross training in combat is still thought of as heresy in some quarters of the martial arts world.

Other books and videos by Geoff Thompson:

Watch My Back – A Bouncer's Story
Bouncer (sequel to *Watch My Back*)
On the Door – *Further Bouncer Adventures*.
The Pavement Arena
– *Adapting Combat Martial Arts to the Street*
Real Self-defence
Real Head, Knees & Elbows
Real Punching
Real Kicking
The Fence
The Art of Fighting Without Fighting
Dead Or Alive – *Self-protection*
3 Second Fighter – The Sniper Option
Weight Training – For the Martial Artist
Animal Day – Pressure Testing the Martial Arts
Tuxedo Warrior:
Tales of a Mancunian Bouncer, by Cliff Twemlow,
foreword by Geoff Thompson
Small Wars - How To Live a Stress Free Life
Fear – The Friend of Exceptional People: techniques in
controlling fear
Blue Blood on the Mat
by Athol Oakley, foreword by Geoff Thompson
Give Him To The Angels
– *The Story Of Harry Greb* by James R Fair
The Art of Fighting Without Fighting
 – *Techniques in threat evasion*

The Ground Fighting Series (books):
Vol. One   – Pins, the Bedrock
Vol. Two   – Escapes
Vol. Three – Chokes and Strangles
Vol. Four – Arm Bars and Joint Locks
Vol. Five – Fighting From Your Back
Vol. Six   – Fighting From Neutral Knees

Videos:
Lessons with Geoff Thompson
Animal Day – Pressure Testing the Martial Arts
Animal Day Part Two – The Fights
Three Second Fighter – The Sniper Option
Throws and Take-Downs Vols. 1-6
Real Punching Vols. 1-3
The Fence

The Ground Fighting Series (videos):
Vol. One   – Pins, the Bedrock
Vol. Two   – Escapes
Vol. Three – Chokes and Strangles
Vol. Four – Arm Bars and Joint Locks
Vol. Five – Fighting From Your Back
Vol. Six   – Fighting From Neutral Knees

Advanced Ground Fighting Vols. 1-3
Pavement Arena Part 1
Pavement Arena Part 2   – The Protection Pyramid
Pavement Arena Part 3   – Grappling, The Last Resort
Pavement Arena Part 4   – Fit To Fight

Contents

Introduction

Why Grappling?

Grappling, it would seem, has always lain hidden within the shadow of popular combat due to its unembellished demeanour, its devastating potency cloaked by a dishevelled curtain; people, naturally, being drawn more to the neon lighted, superfluously spectacular kicking arts.

The world of combat, more specifically the world of Martial Arts has now evolved and superfluousness has failed the acid test of time, unfortunately, in most cases the prettier movements that originally drew thousands like summer moths to a flame balked at the obstacle of practicality proving to be little more than lacklustre. The disreputable and fundamental movements so often ignored due to the 'ugly duckling' syndrome rose above the maelstrom as potentate, the Swan of 'real' combat blossomed leaving the decimated remnants of the former in their wake.

You may feel that my opinion, that of a practising grappler, is biased. I am not 'art prejudiced' though I am very honest. As testimony to the former and latter I feel it is worth recording that two thirds of my qualifications in the world of combat lie in the kicking and punching crafts so it is not just as a grappler that I talk and write, it is as a complete practitioner of the combat arts.

To be a complete exponent it is important that your practice cover all distances so that every possible angle of attack and defence is accounted for. When you consider that 90% of all live combat scenarios end in grappling range and yet less than 10% of combat exponents actually practice or are prepared for the same, something seems acutely amiss.

I have never won, nor for that matter entered, a judo/grappling contest on the controlled arena, (though I have spent many years practising both disciplines). Why then, you will indubitably be asking, should my opinions and writing be so valid? Having spent 20 years of my life arduously practising multifarious fighting arts and 10 years of my life as a professional 'bouncer' applying the same against life's gratuitously Ramboesque minority, I feel pivotally positioned to state categorically what does and does not work. When, why, when not & why not certain techniques should or should not be employed.

Grappling distance differs from any other in that, once sought or found it cannot be exchanged for one more favourable, it is held to the culmination of the fight. When kicking and/or punching you may, if you so desire, for what ever reason, move in and out of the said ranges at will, if you find yourself in grappling range and struggling, you no longer have the option of change because you are held there by the grip of your adversary.

The art of grappling, though by its outer skin it may appear not, is as complex and many splendoured as any other art. It is an apprenticeship, and matriculation is necessary if excellence is to be attained. Its practice is not for the weak willed or faint of heart, though wills and hearts will be dually strengthened by its conscientious practice.

All out grappling on the Judo mat or in the wrestling ring is as close to 'real combat' as you can get, its character building qualities are second to none and for those that stay the course the rewards are immense. The techniques that I endorse herein are derived empirically, their workability has been tested 'in the field'. They are not hypothetical dojo/gym movements.

Real Grappling

I have grappled for my very life on the pavement arena more times than I care to recall, believe me when I tell you that it isn't pleasant.

All of the impending techniques must be practised diligently and the theories adhered to, it is not enough to look at the pictures and learn to 'talk the talk' you have to practice, practice, practice.

Chapter One

A Bit Of History

by Dave Turton 6th dan goshinkwai yawara.

Grappling (wrestling) is probably the oldest genre of combat known to man. Pulling and handling animals was, very likely, the first way, inadvertently, that grappling techniques were used. The natural carrying and pulling strength developed by ancient man was an obvious adjunct to be utilised whilst grappling with foes, animal and human alike.

Most natural acts, i.e. love making, lifting/carrying children, comforting, assisting ill or injured friends or family etc. are close in. Heavy play is, again, a congenital act to man, so it would follow that a degree of grappling skill and strength would automatically develop from this 'play', its transition from this format to actual combat is an inherent and obvious one.

Grappling, unlike most striking arts, can be used for the dual purpose of control and destruction.

EGYPT:
The Beni-Hasan wall paintings, around 3,400 B.C. clearly illustrate wrestling/grappling holds, grips and throws, not unlike those taught in present day gyms and dojo.

Bull wrestling (not to be recommended) was also a very popular spectacle and there seems little doubt that the power needed (and developed) to overcome the awesome might of the bull would be very useful when employing grappling technique against human adversaries.

Real Grappling

Due to the large variety of weaponry openly available in early society unarmed opponent's found the need to develop grappling methods with a design that would help to over come the armed antagonist.

The Greeks and Romans revelled in the art of Wrestling combat, there are examples of this emblazoned up on vases etc. from and throughout this period.

One of the great champions of the day was a formidable gentleman by the name of 'Milo of Craton' who devised the first recorded method of progressive resistance exercise known to man. He carried a bull calf for several hours a day, every day without fail (dumbbells are decidedly easier). As the bull calf grew Milo was lifting and carrying a progressively larger amount every day, his strength pyramiding and soaring with the said increased weight. Eventually, it is said, he could perform his training with a full grown Bull. By this time, not at all surprisingly, he had become the strongest wrestler in all of Greece, he victored in many Olympic games, and other such contests.

The Greeks, under the auspices of Alexander the Great, invaded much of the Mediterranean and Asian lands, including India. It is thought, by several authorities on the matter, that the Greeks introduced their wrestling systems to India, which already had its own indigenous genre of grappling.

Buddhist priests/monks did much travelling through southern China and areas of southern Asia which hints that possibly some Asian combat systems were or are derivations of Greek combat.

The Romans had many grappling methods, in fact one emperor, Commodus, a cruel despotic ruler, victored in over 500 wrestling bouts. He got his just deserts when he was strangled in his sleep by a hired assassin, who was also a professional wrestler.

The Roman invasion of Britain, and subsequent control over this fair land of ours, brought together many systems of unarmed combat.

Throughout the world wrestling and grappling has been a part of EVERY culture, probably due to the fact that, as formerly mentioned, pulling, holding, lifting, carrying etc. are far more natural to us as living, working (not so many of us working these days) human beings than punching or striking.

Toddlers, infants and many young children for example, pull, grab and push far more frequently than they strike, this type of 'inborn combat' is innate, nobody has to teach us these hereditary movements, even Mothers will restrain and chastise their children with holds as opposed to blows.

Mankind's only superior physical asset over the animals and beasts is the thumb, this appendage greatly aids gripping and manipulating, so naturally most combat movements involve grappling. The degree of result is greater for the grappler than for the practitioner who favours striking movements.

The first real mention of Wrestling in the annals of British history is in the ancient 'Book of Leinster' which talks of 'very rough Wrestling in the Tailtin games'. This festival was founded in 1829 B.C. and ended in 554 A.D.

The Greco-Roman system brought by the Romans was in fact considered 'tame' when compared with our Anglo Saxon methods (Which included the Devonians shin kicking whilst wearing horse shoes attached to every day shoes).

In every century from Edward the Confessor's reign (1042-1066) right up to present day, grappling and wrestling is mentioned in historical texts.

In 1564 a team of Cornish Wrestlers severely trounced the French team of 'eleven strong men'. All the country fairs and 'Games' included some form of Wrestling matches, the participants being strong, skilled and brave (they had to be).

Prize fighting and pugilism started to supersede wrestling by the late 18 century, though only because the top prize ring champions were both hitters and grapplers. At the time the 'hitting' was very important within these matches because money was always bet on 'First blood' it was and is always easier to draw blood with a strike as opposed to a throw. However, the bouts were, invariably, won by the better grappler as opposed to the better puncher.

JUDO . . . ASIA

Wrestling in Japan is as ancient an art as any grappling combat system anywhere in the world, its first recorded instance being in 23 B.C. the champion, Sukune.

In 838 the two sons of the emperor Buntoku wrestled each other for the right to the throne, the winner being Koreshito.

By the 17th century grappling had split into two main branches, the sport of Sumo and the many combat systems generally termed as Ju-Jitsu, the latter coming under such names as Yawara-Kempo, Shin no shido ryu and many others. Their integral and original use was for the one-on-one battle field grappling, if one or more had lost a weapon. Due to the restrictive and protective factors of the then worn armour it was usually more useful and therefore effective to throw an adversary than to attempt to strike him.

It is thought that the Chinese probably influenced native Japanese combat grappling during the many trade fares of the 17th century.

One man, a Chinese by the name of Chin-Gen-Pin taught many Samuri his grappling methods. Okayama Hochirojo is credited with founding the tenshin-shido-ryu system which specialised in atemi striking to disable and kill opponents.

In 1882 a 22 year old student/teacher of Ju-Jitsu adapted his knowledge to form Kodokan-Judo, this was Jigoru Kano. He had originally designed the Kodokan as a college to study all the systems of Ju-Jitsu.

During the late Victorian period Yokio Tani came to Britain and performed on the music hall stages taking on all comers. Ju-Jitsu and Judo became well known as excellent methods of grappling defence work. For a long time the two terms/names Judo and Ju-Jitsu were thought of as one and the same.

With international growth came competition and the forming of the B.J.A, the B.J.C. and the A.J.A. It wasn't long before Britain and other countries started beating the Japanese in open contest. Anton Geesink caused a major upset by becoming the first occidental to win a major competition beating the Japanese.

By 1964 Judo became an Olympic sport transcending its roots in actual combat. Modern day Judo is taught as a jacketed wrestling sport. Despite this transition, Judo, as devised by Kano, still holds many excellent combat methods.

The art of atemi is, now, rarely taught and sadly self defence takes a shaded back seat to competition Judo.

In order to spread their popularity many combat systems, Judo, Karate, boxing, fencing, Kendo and others have all gone the same sorry way.

Chapter Two

Stance

A good stance or posture is very important in grappling if you are to be correctly prepared for combat. A poor posture will relegate your attack and defence to lacklustre, so adherence to the following is imperative.

DEFENSIVE STANCE:

Employed to stop or counter an attack. The defensive stance is, effectively, the same as the natural stance, lowering the hips a little more for the stability necessary to withstand an attack.

LEFT OR RIGHT LEAD STANCE:

This is a variation of the former defensive posture, ideal for block or counter. The left leg (right if reversed) is forward, at a 45 degree angle with the right, and slightly bent for stability.

When practising on the mat with a partner your stance will be constantly changing back and forward from attack to defence. Whilst you are attacking or actively defending be sure to return to a stable stance, never allow your feet to cross in movement, to do so will greatly heighten your vulnerability to attack due to impaired balance and bad posture. Never let your feet meet, this again will impair balance and cause top heaviness.

Practice all of the prescribed stances with a partner by taking a grip on each other's attire and moving forward, backwards and around the mat until confidence in stance is found.

Chapter Three

Grips

There are many decreed ways of taking a grip up on an adversary, once a grip is chosen it is not easily traded for another. In the street scenario grappling is not (or shouldn't be) sought and generally you have to take whatever grip you can get and make the best of it.

For the sake of practice and explanation we shall work with the conventionals.

You may grip opposite lapels, opposite lapel and sleeve, neck of jacket and opposite sleeve, or neck of jacket and opposite neck of jacket.

All of the aforementioned, or derivatives thereof, may be successfully employed.

Keep a firm yet relaxed grip, elbows lightly bent. For the street scenario keep your chin to your chest, this will act as protection against possible head butts. Where it is impossible or impractical to grip the opponent's attire you may, instead, grip his limbs, at the wrist, elbow, ankle, between the legs, under the armpits, around the thigh, waist, back, neck or head, depending entirely up on the throw/attack that you chose to employ.

The Catch-as-catch-can method of gripping is to place your arms around the opponent's waist or torso, coupling your hands together by gripping opposite wrists or fingers to strengthen the hold.

Here are a few illustrations of the grips:

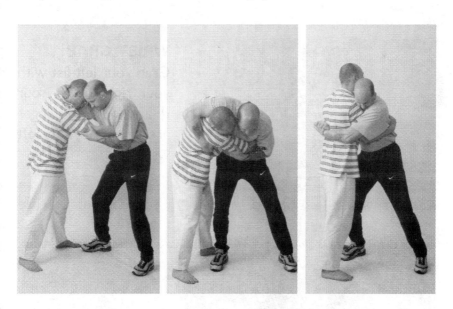

Never intertwine your fingers, when you pull them apart it is easy to dislocate your own knuckles.

GRAB FINGER GRIP:
Grab the four fingers of your left hand with the four fingers of your right hand. Lock them by closing your fists together firmly. Pull on all of your fingers at the same time.

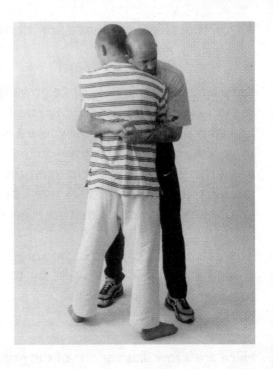

WRIST GRAB:
Grab your left fist with your right hand. Your thumb and middle finger are around your left wrist.

GRAB BACK OF HAND AND WRIST:

Grab your left hand with your right hand. The thumb of your right hand is on the same side as your fingers. The middle finger is in the notch of your left wrist. To make the grip effective you must squeeze harder with the hand that is on top.

Chapter Four

Vertical Grappling

Vertical grappling offers the opportunity to attack an opponent with certain chosen hand strikes or choke/head lock him to unconsciousness without actually going to ground work. Kicks, knees, butts, bites and other atemi may also be used to good effect, all using the grip as an aid for leverage.

BUTTING:

One of the most effective techniques available if used correctly, if used incorrectly can be as dangerous to the bestower as to the recipient. The key factor in the success of the head butt is to keep the attack below the opponent's eye line, anywhere above the eye line is potentially dangerous for the 'butter'.

You may attack with the head in one of five ways:

1. From right to left, using the left corner of your forehead to attack.

2. From left to right, using the right corner of your head to attack.

3. A forward thrusting butt using either the left, centre or right of your forehead to attack.

4. You may attack upward with the crown of your head.

5. You may thrust backward attacking with the back of your head.

All are close range attacks that may be employed with or without the appendage of your hands to pull. In context with the nature of this text we shall be using the hands as pulling implements to aid the butt.

Beside the pulling factor, which generates a lot of potency within the butt, most of the power is derived from, and indeed relies upon a combination of two things, a) pitching the body forward slightly before the head, forcing the head to follow creating the whiplash effect, and b) the propelling body weight, which should still be travelling forward as the head strikes its target, thus adding momentum to the head butt.

LEFT TO RIGHT:

Propel the body forward followed by the head. The right corner of your forehead whiplashes in to the side or front of the recipient's nose, face or jaw. Pull your opponent, via your grip, rapidly toward the head butt.

FORWARD THRUSTING HEAD BUTT:

Propel the body directly forward followed by the front of your head (forehead) whiplashing it in to the opponent's nose, eyes or jaw. Care should be taken when attacking directly from the front not to hit the opponent's teeth, although it would be very painful to the recipient it is also, due to the obvious sharpness of the teeth, dangerous to the attacker. Pull the opponent, via your grip, rapidly towards the butt.

RIGHT TO LEFT:

Propel the body forward followed by the head. The left corner of your forehead whiplashes in to the side or front of the recipient's nose, face or jaw. Pull the opponent, via your grip, rapidly towards the head butt.

UPWARD HEAD BUTT:

Generally employed when your forehead is in the region of your opponent's chest. From this position thrust upward, rapidly attacking your opponent's chin with the front crown of your head.

REVERSE HEAD BUTT:

To be executed when the opponent is standing (or lying) directly behind you or is holding you in a rear bear hug. In the case of the former, propel the body rapidly backwards followed directly by your head, whiplashing the back of your skull in to the opponent's face. In the case of the latter where your body weight is locked in the bear hug position and there for redundant, bring your head slightly forward then throw it backward rapidly, striking the opponent's face with the back of your skull.

BITING:

Biting in combat may seem, to the more squeamish amongst us, an unsavoury and barbaric act: they are right on both counts. Its extreme effectiveness outweighs both points.

To bite or not to bite, that (it would seem) is the question. Many may find the thought of biting an adversary quite repugnant, however, in a street scenario when you are being attacked unsolicitously and your life is, or may be, on the line it loses its repugnance, unsavouriness and barbaric tendencies at a rate of knots emerging from the cocoon of all three as a life saving tactic in the savage 20th century.

From my long experience I have concluded that, in the majority of cases, a bitten adversary is a beaten adversary, even the most ardent of foes capitulate readily to its (the bite) pain inducing qualities, and those that do not submit will remember 'the biter' for the rest of their lives.

There is not a great deal to be taught about biting that isn't already instinctive, natural and obvious. For best results bite the protruding parts of the opponent's anatomy, more specifically the nose, lips and ears, if the opportunity arises (and I hope that it never does) the male private parts, if your assailant is female, the breasts and nipples.

If you do decide to employ the bite don't make it too obvious or the opponent will easily avoid your attempt. Position your mouth as close to the chosen target as possible with out making your intentions obvious, then attack/bite fiercely gripping with your teeth as tightly as possible. Whether you hold the bite or sever (ear, nose etc) is entirely up to you and on the gravity of the situation that you find yourself in.

Use the grip that you have up on the opponent's attire to hold him steady until a secure bite is attained. Once the bite is on the grip on his clothing will become secondary. Nine times out of ten a good bite will place you in complete control of your assailant and the situation, securing victory. A strong minded, stubborn or reticent adversary (there aren't many, but I think I've fought them all. See Watch My Back) will not balk to the pain of your bite, with this minority you may be forced to sever the ear, nose etc.

Be very wary of plea bargaining attackers who will offer the earth and all with in it to be freed from your bite. Their ploy is often to feign capitulation then as soon as you release your bite continue their attack up on you with added ferociousness.

If you are in the mood for a little bargaining and decide to release your bite make sure that you get to your feet (in vertical grappling you will already be standing but if you employ the same bites during ground work get to your feet whilst still retaining the bite) then bite hard before you release. This last infliction of pain up on your foe will give you valuable extra seconds to flee.

As formerly mentioned, the gravity of the situation in which you find yourself largely dictates the usage of biting techniques. I only bite as a last resort, when all else has failed or is not available. You may wish to introduce biting earlier on in the play, the choice is a personal one, though to discard the bite completely when it might well prove to be life saving would be fool hardy.

HAND STRIKES:

It is possible to attack an opponent, directly from any given grip, with short, sharp hand techniques. Due to the close proximity of the attacking hand and the target, (opponent's face/body) power in the chosen strike is not easily attainable, though the forecoming, prescribed strikes require only the minimum of power to be effective, sharpness and accuracy are more important and more accessible from such a short range.

The eyes and jaw are the choice targets for this genre of hand strike.

The eyes: with accuracy an opponent can be 'stopped' in his tracks.

The jaw: even from such a short range, again with a telling strike, an adversary can be disorientated, enough for you to advance with a more telling blow, (choke or throw) or even 'stopped'.

All of the forecoming techniques may be executed left or right handed, my suggestion is that the hand you strike with should be the one that offers most accessibility and power from the position you find yourself in, this should be launched from a small, compact, 45 degree front stance (orthodox or southpaw, depending up on which hand you wish to employ as strike). For accessibility to these strikes the attacking hand is best situated high on the opponent's collar or shoulder.

PRACTICE:

From the vertical grappling position, both partners grip each other's apparel. Due to the close proximity of the target (head) the chosen technique should explode as opposed to being pushy. The desired explosive action is generated by thrusting your right hip (left if employing left hand strikes) sharply behind the chosen movement.

CLAW STRIKE:

From the right collar grip punch your right hand at the opponent's exposed eyes, simultaneously explode your right hip behind and in the same direction as the strike. Form the shape of a claw with the attacking hand just prior to its contact with the opponent's eyes. Attack one or both eyes.

SINGLE FINGER STRIKE:

Should be employed in a direct facsimile to the claw strike, using the index finger as weapon as opposed to the claw hand. Pull the thumb and other three fingers in to a fist.

COUPLED FINGER STRIKE:

Should be employed in a direct facsimile to the claw/index finger strike, using all of the fingers and thumb to strike as opposed to the claw/index finger. Couple all the fingers together to form the shape of a bird's beak, collectively aim all at one chosen eye (whichever is most accessible).

PALM HEEL STRIKE:

Again, used in a technical facsimile to the forgoing strikes using the palm heel as opposed to the fingers as weapon, and targeting the opponent's jaw as opposed to his/her eyes. Pull your hand and fingers back as taught as is possible, attack with the heel of the hand. Strike the jaw bone on the curve for best effect.

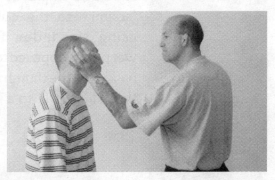

SNATCH & ATTACK:

All of the forgoing attacks may be employed as described or utilising the power generating snatch & attack method which is particularly effective when the opponent is gripping the sleeve of the arm that you wish to employ as strike. Snatch your arm back violently breaking the grip of your opponent, use the snatched arm to attack the opponent's eyes, jaw or throat.

ELBOW STRIKES:

From the vertical grappling position it is difficult to use the elbows as attacking tools, though not impossible. Using the snatch & attack method formerly described, mawashi empi (round house elbow strike) can be very effective. After snatching and breaking the opponent's grip attack, using the point of the elbow (right or left) his face/jaw in a semi-circular manner thrusting your right hip behind and in the same direction as the blow.

ELBOW DROP:

From a tight lapel grip relax your arms and suddenly thrust your right (or left) elbow in to your opponent's front ribs, driving your right hip behind and in the same direction as the elbow strike (left hip if employing the left elbow). Don't release your lapel grip, use it for leverage by pulling out wards on the lapel as the point of the elbow sinks in to the opponent's body.

CHOKES & HEADLOCKS:

A good choke/headlock, if employed correctly is a definite stopping technique, usually (and easily) rendering your opponent unconscious. Very accessible with a low skill factor.

Several of the strangles/chokes use the opponent's jacket or shirt as an aid for leverage, whilst others (naked strangles/chokes) work independently of the opponent's attire.

The following movements are equally effective whilst in the vertical or horizontal position.

When familiarity with chokes and strangles is found it is possible and probable that one movement may flow in to another giving you a bastardisation of your own invention or design, this is acceptable and encouraged, as long as the new movement is effective.

The function of the strangle is to cut off the opponent's blood supply and subsequently the oxygen, to the brain, by compressing the Carotid arteries either side of the neck. The function of the choke is to cut off the oxygen supply to the brain by compressing the wind pipe. Former or latter will induce unconsciousness within seconds. All of the following chokes/strangles can prove fatal so, in practice be careful. ALWAYS employ the 'tap' system.

REVERSE NAKED CHOKE:

This particular choke is usually executed from the opponent's rear, with a little added skill it may also be employed from the front. For effective use from the front the right hand is best located gripping the opponent's attire by his left shoulder, your left hand, anywhere on his right.

Push your right hand sharply forward, forcing the opponent's body to twist around. Release your right grip and quickly place your right arm around and across the opponent's throat, clasp your right hand with your left and apply pressure to the throat by pulling backward with the combined force of both arms. For maximum effect make sure that the bony part of the right wrist is against the throat as opposed to the softer forearm. It also helps at this point if you can pull the opponent backwards and off his feet, this lessens the opponent's 'fight back' chances.

SIDE HEAD LOCK/ STRANGLE:

Release your grip of the opponent's left lapel and place your right arm around the opponent's neck, hugging his neck and head tightly down in to the side of your own body. The palm of your right fist should, at this point be facing inwards so that the bony part of your right wrist is digging in to the opponent's neck. Place your left palm heel underneath your  right fist and apply pressure on the opponent's neck/cartoid, pushing up with the left hand and squeezing in with the right.

GUILLOTINE LIFT:

Release your grip on the opponent's left lapel. Push your entire right arm past the right side of his face whilst pulling him forward with your left hand, via his attire, forcing, and hugging, his head under your right arm pit. Slide your right arm under and across his throat. Your right fist palm should be facing in to your own body to ensure that the bony part of the wrist is digging in to the opponent's throat. Place your left palm heel under the right fist and apply pressure on the throat by pushing the right arm up and in to the throat with the left hand whilst simultaneously pulling the right arm in to the throat.

CLAW SQUEEZE AROUND THE LARYNX:

Release your grip on the opponent's left lapel and quickly grip the opponent's larynx, which is situated at the top of the wind pipe, just below the chin, squeeze tightly.

The larynx grab is more effective if your opponent has his back to a wall or to the floor.

SCISSOR CHOKE:

Release your left and right grip of the opponent's attire, cross your hands with palms facing downwards and grab the opponent's lapels as deeply to the back of the neck as possible (right hand to the opponent's right lapel, left hand to the opponent's left lapel). Apply pressure to the neck by pushing both elbows, simultaneously, downwards, forcing both wrists in to either side of the opponent's neck.

KNEES:

To the groin or testicles this is a simple but effective technique. Lift the knee upwards as quickly as possible. A slow pushy movement would prove to be ineffective, the quicker the ascent of the attacking knee the greater the impact. Pull downwards on the opponent's attire as you lift the knee for greater effect. If applying the same technique to the opponent's head or face first release your lapel grip and grab the opponent's head by the hair, ears or by coupling the fingers of both hands at the back of his skull and pull his head down rapidly towards your attacking knee, simultaneously bring the attacking knee rapidly upward to meet the descending head/face. As the former and latter meet smash the head through he knee.

FORWARD KNEE:

Much the same technique as the thrusting front kick, using the knee as opposed to the foot as the attacking tool. Relies heavily up on the grip you have up on the opponent. Aggressively pull the opponent, via his attire, rapidly toward your attacking knee. Simultaneously thrust the attacking knee (left or right) upward and forward to meet the opponent's body on its decent. At the moment of impact thrust both hips forward, behind the knee, thrusting it in to the opponent's body, whilst still pulling downward with the grip.

ROUND HOUSE KNEE:

Much the same as the round house kick, using the knee as the attacking tool as opposed to the foot. Again this attack is more effective when combined with the 'pulling' qualities of the grip. May be used effectively to the opponent's knee, thigh or body.

To the knee, thigh or body lift the attacking knee up and away from your body then thrust it downward and in to the target, simultaneously pull the opponent, via his attire, toward the attacking knee. On impact thrust your hips forward and drop your weight in to the technique.

FEET:

By nature of the very close proximity of grappling range kicks do not, because they cannot, play a major roll. It is relegated to two effective techniques, one a weakener, the other a possible 'finisher'.

SHIN KICK:

The shin kick, as the title suggests, is a very simple kick to the opponent's shin. This attack is a weakener or 'connecting' attack (a small attack designed to distract the opponent long enough to make an opening for a larger more substantial attack). If you are wearing tough shoes it can be a very pain inflicting tactic that will cause, at the very least, the said distraction.

KIN GERI:

Kin geri is a front snap kick aimed at the testicles using the instep of the foot as the attacking tool. From a small, left leading stance draw your left leg back, keeping your head and shoulders tightly tucked in to the opponent's head and shoulders, kick your right leg sharply between the opponent's legs. If the opponent's legs are not open wide enough to permit the passage of your foot you may attack in the same way aiming the ball of your foot in to the opponent's pubic bone.

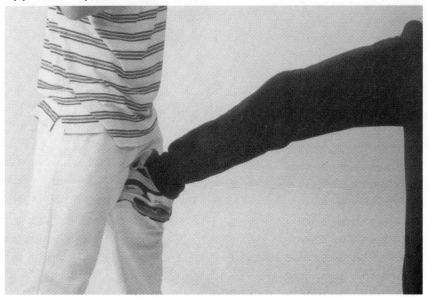

ANKLE STAMP:

From a natural stance lift your left or right knee up and 'stamp', using the heel of your foot as the attacking tool, on to the opponent's left or right ankle.

All of the foregoing techniques may be effectively used in the live scenario. In the controlled arena (the dojo, gym) they must, for obvious reasons, be practised with observed control if serious injury is to be avoided.

The other obvious attack from the horizontal posture is the throw. This is covered in greater detail in the next chapter.

Chapter Five

Throws

A good throw can be spectacular and effective and for the advanced Judoki or Wrestler very accessible. To the novice accessibility to throwing techniques is dulled by the very high skill factor that is demanded in pursuit of competence. The throw is far more effective (to the advanced or novice) if preceded by a strike (head butt, hand strike, bite etc.) Often, as a singular attack, the throw can be neutralised, even by a strong novice. If, however, you precede the throw with a strike, bite, butt etc. the success rate of the throw elevates markedly. This concept is out of the context of this particular chapter which specialises in the singular throw, in a later chapter, 'Combinations', it is covered in depth. For now it is better to master the fundamentals of the throw before attempting to combine with other attacking tools.

Throws vary in suitability to different body types, whilst most throws may be utilised by most people some do suit certain body types more than others. The only real way to ascertain a throw's suitability to you as an individual is to try it out in the controlled arena. Discard those that do not suit and build on those that do, make them your own.

There are a myriad of throws that fall in to three categories: foot throws, hip throws, and shoulder throws, with a few odd scatterings in between.

The more complex movements would be inapplicable (to the beginner) in the street scenario, in this arena only basic is synonymous with effective. Bastardisations of the throwing techniques may be, intentionally or unintentionally, sought and executed, as long as they are effective.

The Sacrifice throw, as taught in many grappling disciplines, where the thrower sacrifices his own safety in a last ditch attempt at throwing his opponent is not a throw that I would recommend for the 'live' scenario, you could quite easily end up with more injuries than the person that you are attempting to throw. For this reason I have not included any with in this text. Throws can be executed with or without the aid of the opponent's clothing for grip. Where the opponent's clothing is too flimsy to use as leverage, or not available, use the opponent's limbs for grip, or where applicable wrap your arms around the opponent's neck or torso to assist you in the chosen throw.

MAJOR OUTER REAPING THROW:

From the conventional lapel/sleeve grip this throw is both simple and highly effective, though relies (as do all throws) on a fast explosive attack.

Break the opponent's balance backward to the right corner as you simultaneously advance your left foot forward. Continue to draw the opponent's balance outward as you reap your right leg to the back of the opponent's right leg throwing him backwards. To make the throw a little more gratuitous you may release your right hand grip of the opponent's lapel and grab him under the chin, as you reap his leg to throw simultaneously shove his head backwards, in the same direction as he is falling. To attack to the opponent's left side reverse the instructions.

HIP THROW:

Break the opponent's balance forward to the right front corner as you simultaneously advance your right foot towards the opponent's right foot. Make a body turning in entry and place your right arm around the opponent's waist (neck or under his armpit). Make sure that both of your feet are inside the opponent's, your bottom tightly in to his groin and your knees bent. Throw the opponent forward fast and explosively over your hip. May be reversed. This throw works equally well with or without the added leverage of the opponent's apparel.

MAJOR INNER REAPING:

Break the opponent's balance backward as you simultaneously reap your right leg through and around the inside opponent's lower left leg, lifting the leg off the ground. Push the opponent (or butt him) violently backwards. May be reversed.

SHOULDER THROW:

Break the opponent's balance forward as you simultaneously advance your right foot toward his right foot. Make a body turning in movement as you pass your right arm under the opponent's right armpit, gripping hold of his attire. Try to keep both of your feet inside your opponent's and bend at the knees, (you may even drop to your knees) throw the opponent over your right shoulder fast and explosively. May be reversed.

MINOR OUTER REAPING ANKLE THROW:

Break the opponent's balance to his right back corner as you simultaneously advance your left foot forward followed by your right foot. Reap the back of the opponent's right heel with your right foot, push (or butt) him violently backwards. If the opponent's feet are very close together you may, with a little more effort, sweep both his legs at once by attacking his left heel thus catching both of his legs at once.

SWEEPING ANKLE THROW:

Advance your right foot forward forcing your opponent backward on to his left foot. Take a wide left step as you advance your right foot inward to support your body weight. Break the opponent's balance to the right side and simultaneously sweep his feet together as you lift him upward. Throw him with speed and force. May be reversed.

BODY DROP THROW:

Break the opponent's balance to his right front corner. Advance your right foot towards the opponent's right foot. Position your body so that your right foot blocks the opponent's right ankle whilst your left leg is bent. As you throw the opponent directly forward and over the back of your right ankle, with speed and force, straighten your left leg to aid the throw. If the opponent is wearing a tie or scarf you may grab the said garment with your right hand and use it to pull the opponent over your ankle. Where no garment is available to hold place your right arm around the opponent's neck or grab his hair and pull him in the direction of the throw.

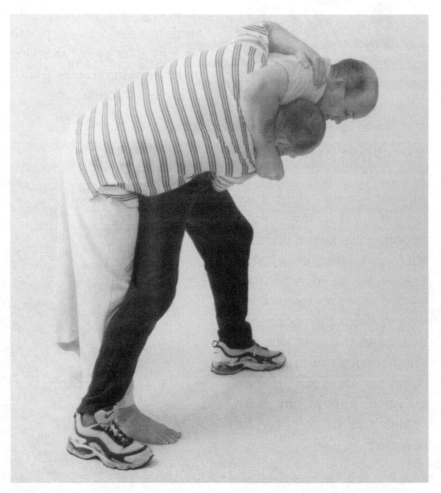

SWEEPING HIP THROW:

Break the opponent's balance to the right front corner and simultaneously advance your right foot toward the opponent's right foot. Continue to swing your body in to position so that the left foot is positioned in the centre of gravity. Place your right arm around the opponent's waist or neck. Sweep the back of your right thigh against the front of the opponent's right thigh. Continue sweeping backward and throw the opponent directly forward and over your thigh. May be reversed.

INNER THIGH THROW:

Break the opponent's balance forward to his right front corner. Advance your right foot toward the opponent's right foot. Make a body turning in movement so that your left foot is positioned in the centre of gravity. Place your right arm around the opponent's waist or neck. Sweep your right thigh upward on the inside of the opponent's left thigh. Continue sweeping up and back. Throw the opponent directly forward and over your right thigh with force and speed. May be reversed.

FIREMAN'S LIFT (FROM KNEES):

Drop in to a crouch position, right side on (left if reversed) and at right angles with your opponent. Drive your right arm between the opponent's legs and grip or lock on around and behind the opponent's right thigh.

Simultaneously place your right foot between his feet. With your left hand grip the opponent's right arm or sleeve, this grip is used to pull the opponent down and across your shoulders. As the opponent's feet leave the mat/floor you should slip him over your head by dipping it down sharply to the mat, simultaneously straightening your legs form the crouched position. Throw the opponent to the floor, or alternatively, as you drop the opponent, go on to one knee so that he lands, back first, on the point of your other knee.

LEG LIFT:

Lower your hips and prepare to move in under his centre of gravity. Scoop his legs up with your hands so that his body lifts and drops backwards to the floor.

There are of course many other throws that are basically the same as the forgoing with minor grip or stance changes that do not need illustrating in this text, the are merely bastardisations of those shown.

For the mat or contest arena, where fine detail may be pivotal in the winning or losing of a match these small changes are important, on the 'pavement' it is the solid grounding in basic technique that is potentate.

It is commonly known that the neophyte grappler can be confused or thrown easier with a solid fundamental throw than with grip variations and feints, the novice grappler/man on the street has no comprehension of these advanced concepts so, logically, will not be drawn by them. On the mat where two evenly matched opponents neutralise each other, tricks and feints are an imperative part of the fighter's curriculum. If he strives to victor against the mugger/attacker on the street the 'neutralising factor' does not arise so there is no need for tricks or feints, a butt or strike is enough to distract an adversary long enough for you to execute your throw.

Sometimes, depending up on the calibre (weight, strength etc) of the adversary facing you, the singular throw will work on its own merits. If the said throw is well rehearsed and explosive the adversaries natural defence mechanism will not have time to 'click in' and neutralise your attempt, it is usually only the lacklustre or telegraphed throw that allows him to pre-empt you with a sudden surge of resisting power. Obviously not every one can gain such perfection in a throw, so, at the risk of repeating myself, pre-empt the throw with a strike, just in case.

All of the forgoing (as with all new techniques) should be practised with an opponent who, initially, offers no resistance. When competence in the technique is obtained light resistance may be offered, pyramiding to full resistance when you feel completely confident with the throw.

Chapter Six

Ground Work

Ground work is split in to two categories:

1) Grappling on the floor.

2) Fighting from the floor.

The former is when you and your partner both fall to the floor, the latter, when you fall/are knocked to the floor and your opponent is still in the vertical position.

Both are dangerous fighting areas to find yourself in, especially the latter. Some schools of thought advocate the latter as first line attack, advising their students to throw themselves to the floor before an adversary and attack/fight from there. This is foolhardy and dangerous, even if you are an experienced ground fighter, and tantamount to throwing yourself at the mercy of your attacker, after all, isn't that (on the floor) where he wants you in the first place?

No! Any form of ground work should be avoided at all costs, whenever possible.

It would be easy, again, for me to show illustrations and demonstrations of how a felled opponent may attack and break an advancing assailant's shin or kneecap with a low line thrust kick or, sweep him to the ground with a leg scissor throw when, in reality, if you are on the ground and your attacker is standing your chances, as a novice, of getting back up again are minimal. Even an experienced fighter is facing defeat if he finds himself 'on the floor'.

If both you and your opponent/assailant fall to the ground you have a far better chance of surviving the altercation or winning. If you do find yourself, singularly, on the floor your vertical assailant will definitely 'go in for the kill'. So it is imperative that you, the defender, quickly secure a good defensive posture, this may be lying on your side, left or right (as illus) where, if you'll note, both arms and legs are being used to provide support enabling quick movement and position change. The right knee and right elbow (left if reversed) are easily available to provide cover for the body, groin or head. From this position hook one foot behind the attacker's advancing foot to give you leverage then thrust your right foot into and through the attacker's shin. Get to your feet whilst he is recovering, if he persists before you can get to your feet kick out rapidly at his groin, knees or shins every time he comes with in range.

Always, as soon as is humanly possible get back up! Only ever fight form the floor when you have no other option open to you.

Never choose ground fighting strategies when vertical alternatives are available.

SITTING UP:
Again notice how the left leg and knee completely protect the groin and body whilst the left arm and elbow is ideally positioned to protect the head and face, it is also well placed to block oncoming kicks.

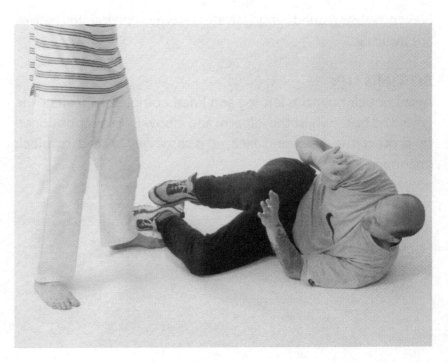

Parry the opponent's attacks until you can get back up from the ground. If you are finding this an impossible task try to catch hold of the attacker's arms or legs and pull him to the floor where you will have a more even chance. If you have to 'take' blows the legs and arms are the best place to do so because they protect the major organs. However, PAIN is a major by-product of 'taking it': grit your teeth and be stoical until you either find your feet (they're at the end of your legs) or topple your assailant.

If you both fall to the floor it is important that you fight back hard and fiercely by striking the opponent in his vital areas, eyes, throat, groin etc. Try to make your attacks calculated and accurate, don't waste time and energy by attacking the less vulnerable, muscularly protected areas of the body such as the chest and back. Energy levels dissipate rapidly at this range, only expend it on useful, pain inducing attacks. Bite, pinch, gouge, butt, knee, choke, do anything and everything.

All of the forgoing described attacks (in chapter five) prescribed for VERTICAL GRAPPLING will work equally well (better in some instances) in horizontal grappling, but be warned, don't expect your assailant to let you put the moves 'on' him, you'll have to fight tooth and nail to be effective, paradoxically, one good choke, gouge or lock will win you the fight.

The following techniques are all useful whilst 'on the ground' but remember, they are only guidelines, you should 'change to suit', these moves are not set in concrete. There is only one rule when it comes to technique, if it works, use it. There are more techniques available than the following recommendations but most would be impractical for the street scenario, for this reason they are not included herein.

SCARF HOLD:

Sit at your opponent's right side, (left if reversed) lean across his chest and place your right arm around/under his neck, take a firm grip on his attire with the same hand. Wrap the opponent's right arm firmly around your own waist and hold his sleeve with your left hand keeping it firmly in place. Keep your right knee bent and close to your opponent's right shoulder and your left leg slightly behind you and straight.

FRONT CHIN-TO-CHEST NECK CRANK:

Sit on your opponent's stomach, pinning his shoulders with your knees as a controlling factor. Turn his head sideways. Grab the back of his head and pull it toward your stomach, forcing his chin into his own chest.

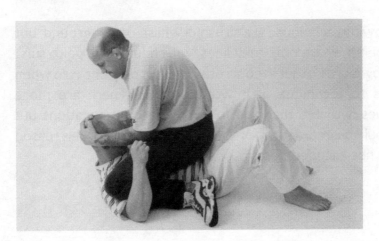

A STOCKS, SIT OUT AND FORWARD NECK CRANK:

You and your opponent are facing each other, both at knee level. Grab your opponent's right arm above the elbow with your left hand. Pull him close to you forcing his head to the right side of your body. Drive your right arm underneath his left arm and around his back. Raise your right foot into a driving position and turn to your left forcing him onto his back. Keep your left grip on his right elbow, locking the arm into the side of your body. Your right hand/arm is behind his neck and underneath his left arm. Place your right palm on the mat/floor as you lean back and bring your legs forward. The back of your right arm will force his head forward and his chin into his own chest. The more you lean back, the more pressure it applies to the opponent's neck.

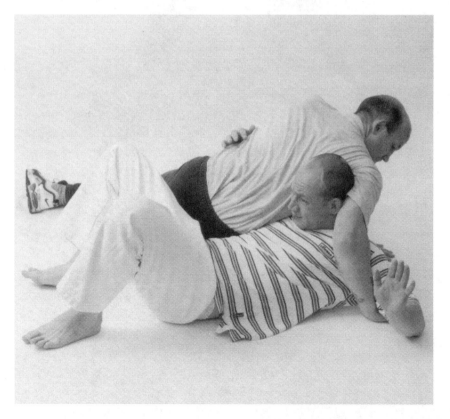

FORWARD FIGURE-4 HOLD DOWN:

Lying on top of your opponent, feed your left arm around the back of his neck. Grab your right bicep with your left hand, making sure that his chin is resting on your left shoulder. Squeeze tightly and lean forward. As you squeeze, the pressure on the thumb side of your left wrist presses against the back of your opponent's neck.

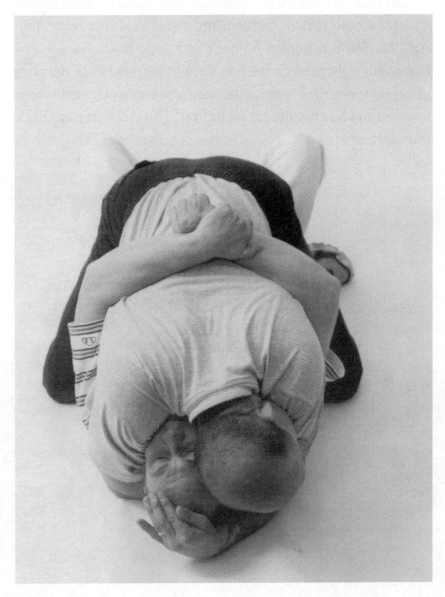

SHOULDER HOLD AND NECK CHOKE:

Your opponent is on his back. Feed your left arm around his neck, push his left arm over his head with the top of your head, push your head against the outside of his left arm and head. Pull your left arm, palm down, with your right hand, palm up. Pull your right elbow toward your stomach, tightening the choke on the backside of his neck. The thumb side of your left wrist slides across the right side of his neck, stemming the blood flow to his brain.

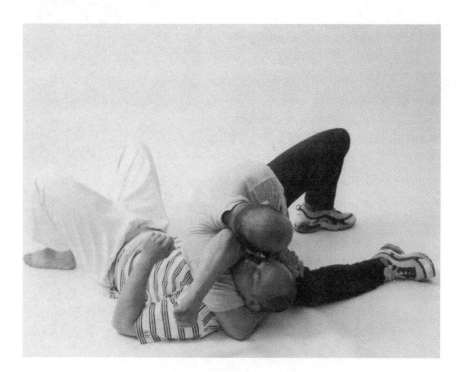

ARM HUG ELBOW LOCK. (Whilst lying on back):

Wrap your arms around your opponent's straight left arm pulling his body close to you, your right knee bent and pushing against the left side of your opponent's body. His left arm is extended and his wrist is on your shoulder, pressing against the right side of your neck. Grip your left wrist with your right hand, forcing the thumb side of your left wrist against and right above his left elbow. Rotate his elbow slightly to your left locking it, this increases the pressure on the joint as you straighten and lock your opponent's elbow.

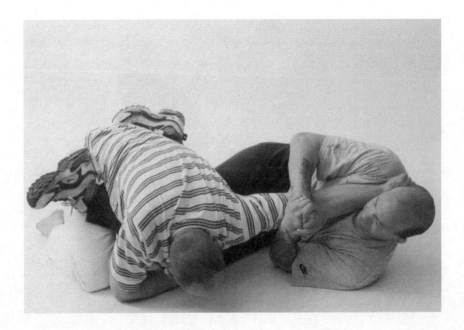

REVERSE SCARF HOLD:

This is a reverse of the traditional scarf hold. Sit with your legs spread widely (left leg forward, right leg back). Feed your left hand under the opponent's left shoulder and grip his attire at waist level. Grip his right forearm under your right armpit, his right sleeve with the same hand to keep the arm in place. Lay back slightly, trapping the opponent's head. Make sure that your weight bears down upon the opponent's chest. If you lean back more you will force your torso weight onto the opponent's face and throat causing a smothering effect.

UPPER FOUR QUARTERS HOLD:

Lie face down with the top of your head facing towards the opponent's feet and with chests touching. Take both of your arms under the opponent's shoulders and grip his attire at the waist with both hands, one either side. Do not lay too high on the opponent's chest, you should hold with both elbows pinched under the opponent's shoulders. As and if he struggles to escape, keep his body in line with your own and lay with the side of his head pinned to and under your upper chest. For a smothering effect lay your abdomen directly over the opponent's face.

Again, as with the throwing techniques, it is possible to form effective variations of the aforementioned. There are also many others besides those shown in this text. Most of those not demonstrated herein, though effective in the controlled arena, are not practical for use in the uncontrolled arena. It is for this reason that I have not included them, that is not to say that anything not included in this text is not effective, I am sure if you search you will find other suitable holds/throws etc. Many holds not shown herein fail in practicality because the angle and posture in which they are executed has the bestower in a prime position to get back to his feet. I see no point in continuing ground work if you are in a position to get back up and a) run or b) finish your adversary from the vertical position. All the time you are horizontal you are in grave danger, not just from the adversary with whom you are grappling but from his friends and compatriots who will take no pains in destroying you whilst your limbs are tied up in a grappling embrace.

All the foregoing techniques should be practised initially with an opponent who offers no resistance. Once competence is achieved in the basic movement, light resistance may be offered. When you feel confident with the chosen technique, it may be practised with complete resistance.

Chapter Seven

Finger Locks

The last chapter, ground work, offered one or two locks and levers, this chapter is dedicated entirely to the art of finger locks.

Note: A lock is taking a limb to the periphery of its natural movement and then further, a lever is when you take the limb against its natural movement.

In all honesty finger locks and levers do not play major role in the street scenario, they are rainy day techniques. Despite the latter the art of locking must not be slighted, though reverence should be shown to the more realistic movements.

As with all techniques 'finger locks' and do not just 'fall in to place', every throw, hold down, choke and lock has to be hard fought for. Most locks may be employed whilst standing, or grappling on the floor.

FINGERS:
Many of the finger locking techniques lack practicality due to the presence of sweat or blood making them too slippery to hold or grip, if however a grip is obtained it is very easy to break bones in the fingers.

LITTLE FINGER BEND:
Grab the opponent's bent left arm at the wrist with the thumb, ring and little finger of your right hand (left if reversed). Place your middle and index fingers around his little finger and take the slack out slowly by bending his little finger backward. Keep your right upper arm and his left upper arm lodged tightly together.

In practise be very careful, the bones in the fingers break very easily.

TWO FINGER SPREAD:

Grip two of the opponent's left fingers (right if reversed) in each of your hands (from any position that allows) and slowly (or sharply if you want to break the finger off) spread and separate the fingers.

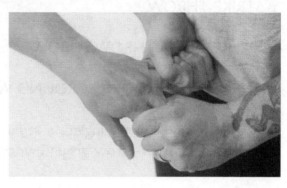

THUMB BEND:

From behind grip the opponent's thumb and pull it sharply backwards. Keep your upper arm and the opponent's upper arm wedged very closely together for better control.

All finger locks, due to the vulnerability and delicateness of the joints, should be practised with/on an opponent who offers little or no resistance. Fully fledged locks should only be practised when the situation demands, ie. real situations.

Chapter Eight

Combinations

Combinations fall in to three categories, and are, in effect, a cocktail of all the forgoing criteria, the categories are thus:

a) STRIKE-THROW.

b) FEINT/FAILED THROW-THROW.

c) THROW-HOLD DOWN/GROUND WORK.

These three may be intermingled, ie. strike-throw-ground work, or strike-feint throw-throw-ground work.etc.

In the following text I shall cover a), b), and c), as listed above, the intermingling of the three is a natural progression and needs little teaching, as confidence is gained one naturally flows one technique in to another, though this is an advanced concept that will only come with much practise. There are an infinite number of variations to the aforementioned, some of which I shall explore shortly, it is not enough to rely up on this text and imprison yourself to its periphery, experiment and explore until you are able to tailor your own metaphoric suit of combinations. If you try a move that doesn't quite suit you, change it so that it does, remember the only rule here is that your deviance be effectual.

All of the forcoming will be listed without in-depth description of the individual movements, for greater detail please refer to the relevant, foregoing chapters (Chapter 5 - Throws, Chapter 4 - Horizontal Grappling) where digression has been undertaken.

STRIKE-THROW:

Almost every available strike may be used with almost every single throw giving you an infinite number of possible variations, the few listed here are appetisers. The 'STRIKE' in the forthcoming combinations is intended to stun the opponent momentarily, giving you vital second to execute the throw, without 'opponent resistance', the sudden infliction of pain from your strike is intended to, and will, draw the opponent's attention long enough for you to explode in to a more consequential technique, this is not to say that the distracting strike may not be effectual on its own merits to finish the fight, very often it is.

Before you attack the opponent with the distracting strike, manoeuvre yourself in to natural stance (feet parallel, shoulder width apart, toes slightly turned inwards) and execute the chosen throw from there. This applies whether you choose to throw left or right sided, at an advanced level you may lead with the side that you wish to throw from (right if throwing right sided etc.) feeding your feet in to prime position before striking and exploding in to a throw. For best effect the throw should follow immediately after the distracting strike, or the opening that you have made will close.

1) head butt - major outer reaping throw.

2) head butt - hip throw.

3) head butt - major inner reaping throw.

4) head butt - forward knee thrust-inner thigh throw.

5) head butt - upward knee thrust-sweeping hip throw.

6) ear bite - forward knee thrust-major inner reaping throw.

7) cheek bite - ankle stamp-inner thigh throw.

8) side head lock - hip throw.

9) upper throat lift - major outer reaping throw.

10) claw squeeze (or strike) around the larynx - shoulder throw.

11) round house knee - major inner reaping throw (to the attacked leg)

12) upward head butt - upward knee strike-body drop throw.

upward head butt

upward knee strike

body drop throw

13) forward head butt-kingeri (groin snap kick) sweeping hip throw.

forward head butt   groin snap kick

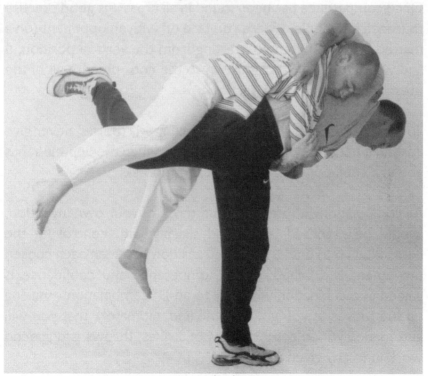

sweeping hip throw

14) neck bite-shin kick-major outer reaping throw.

15) palm heel strike-round house knee-minor outer reaping throw (to the attacked leg).

If you find that, having successfully executed the throw, your opponent maintains his grip and pulls you to the floor with him, you may add, to any given combination, a strike or a hold down as described in earlier chapters, for instance, in combination No. 9, upper throat lift-major outer reaping throw you may add a knee or elbow drop (dropping on to the felled opponent with the point of your knee or elbow, as you fall) to the opponent's exposed head, ribs or groin etc. Combination No 8. Side head lock-hip throw will easily and logically be followed by scarf hold and fist choke whilst on the ground. More probably, if you are pulled to the ground with the opponent you will have to fight for a hold, choke etc. (as described in Chapter 7 - Ground Work). Once competence has been found in all areas it is good practise to free fight grapple, where you face off with an opponent (on a matted area) and grapple, starting from the vertical position, if and when you fall or are thrown to the floor practise all of the prescribed ground work tactics.

To build endurance, stamina and a strong will (bottle) never give in, until it becomes dangerous not to, ie. when the opponent has you in a choke or lock that you cannot break.

All combinations, those listed and those of your own invention, should be practised lightly and sharply with control (in the controlled area) until a smooth transition between each chosen movement is attained. Once competence and confidence is gained in combination work try to ad-lib combinations, making up the moves as you go. You will find, ultimately, that you will automatically feed combinations of strikes, throws and ground work in to any given situation.

FEINT/FAILED THROW-THROW:
On the Judo mat, at an advanced level a player may feint one throw to 'open' his opponent up for another. For example, if you attack with a single throw with the intention of throwing the

opponent in a certain direction (backward, forward, side ways) and he blocks or successfully defends against the said throw, that defence, successful though it may have been, leaves him vulnerable to attack in another direction, usually the opposite direction to which you have just tried to throw him. For instance, a body drop or shoulder throw, which are intended to throw an opponent forward, will if successfully blocked, leave the opponent vulnerable to the major or minor inner and outer reaping throws, which are designed to throw an opponent backwards.

In blocking any given throw the opponent invariably resists by pulling or pushing in the opposite direction to the intended throw. When you attempt to throw him forward with a shoulder throw he will instinctively pull back to resist, momentarily leaving himself vulnerable to the aforementioned reaps, in effect he is throwing himself.

On the mat, facing an opponent who has an understanding of throwing technique the feint concept has a fair chance of working, on the man in the street who has no conception of what a throw is or how he is supposed to react to a feint, it would not. For this reason I feel that feint throws are lost in the street arena, a good, solid, explosive, fundamental throw is superior every time. However, a failed throw (usually they fail when telegraphed) will need a second throw to finish the job. For this reason I shall list a few combinations and ask you to design a few of your own that may suit your body type/temperament more than the cross section that follows.

Be warned: Combining throws is a very advanced concept, much practice and competence in the basic throw must be seen before attempting combination techniques, even then my recommendation is that you use it only as 'back up' and not as a feint. On the Pavement Arena only basic is synonymous with effective.

To make the combination between two throws effective the opening created by the first throw/feint must be filled immediately by the second 'back up' throw or the gap will have closed.

All of the following combinations may be practised/executed left or right sided.

1) major outer reaping throw-sweeping hip throw.

2) major outer reaping throw-inner thigh throw.

major outer reaping throw

3) major outer reaping throw-body drop throw.

body drop throw

4) hip throw-major inner reaping throw.

5) hip throw-minor inner reaping throw.

6) hip throw-major outer reaping throw.

7) hip throw-minor outer reaping throw.

8) sweeping hip throw-major outer reaping throw.

9) sweeping hip throw-minor outer reaping throw.

10) inner thigh throw-major inner reaping throw.

inner thigh throw

major inner reaping throw

Again, the possible number of combinations are almost infinite. More (other than the forgoing) should be sought and practised. To culminate this chapter I should like to underline the previously stated FACT that BASIC is EFFECTIVE. As complication comes through the door, accessibility, usability and effectiveness goes out of the window.

Chapter Nine

Beating The Kicker

If this book was not peripherised in context by its slavery to street effectiveness, then this chapter and the next, beating the puncher, would indeed be a difficult one to pen, involving a myriad of defences against multiple high and low level kicks, a veritable book in itself. As it is, the latter falls outside the purlieus of this text due to the fact that street kicking is very basic, so my job here is thankfully a little easier.

It is true that kickers can be dangerous, though I personally see the kicker (my profuse apologies to all you kicking enthusiasts) as the least dangerous of all fighting adversaries. Even the skilled kicker would find little effect on/in an arena which is, 99% of the time, notoriously close.

To beat the kicker you have to first recognise the needs of the kicker. What does he rely upon to be effective? What are his strengths and weaknesses?

Once discovered the weaknesses should be manipulated and the strengths/needs taken away.

Firstly the kicker relies almost completely on distancing. He needs to be far enough away from you to employ kicking techniques, Secondly he needs a target, generally with the neophyte kicker, this would be the groin or abdomen. The latter target can be taken away simply by turning your body to a 45 degree angle whilst in a compact left lead or right lead stance, depending upon your preference. By angling your body, you minimise the target area, leaving the opponent no vulnerable body parts at which to kick.

The former distance can in theory be taken away from the kicker by moving towards him, closing the gap, he will doubtlessly move back or kick out as you move in to maintain the said gap. This is where the complication lies. To move onto the kick can be very dangerous, not to mention painful, so care must be taken when 'bridging the gap'. Timing is of the essence if you are to avoid being kicked en route and the inevitable cat'n'mouse if the opponent moves back every time you move forward, nothing would be gained and a lot of energy would be expended fruitlessly. For this reason I recommend moving forward when it is impossible or difficult for the kicker to move back. This can be attained in several ways. (All of the following close downs should lead to a grip on the kicker. Once the grip is achieved you may employ any of the attacks in the latter chapters.)

1) Moving forward pre-emptively.

2) Moving forward as he prepares to kick.

3) Catch the kicking leg.

4) Side step.

5) Side step and parry.

6) Moving forward as he retracts the kick.

7) 'Take' the kick and grab.

8) The rush.

All the former may be used with varying degrees of skill and bagfuls of courage. In all but N'8, timing is the pivotal factor.

1) MOVING FORWARD PRE-EMPTIVELY:

Leading with your left or right leg in a 45 degree front stance, edge ever close to your opponent whilst at all times monitoring his every movement. This constant advance will force the kicker to either move backwards to maintain kicking distance or kick out at you to stifle your advance. If you do get close enough to him before he attempts to kick, grab and pull him into grappling range where you may employ any of the attacks described in other chapters. If you do not get close enough, wait for the very first signs of attack, usually a knee lift, lunge forward before the kick gains momentum, grab and pull into grappling range.

2) AS THE OPPONENT KICKS/PREPARES TO KICK:

As with the pre-emptive grab, edge carefully forward and if possible grab and pull the kicker into grappling range. If this is not possible, wait for the opponent to kick. As he does so, move sharply forward, smothering the kick half way, grab and pull him into grappling range. This approach requires a lot of skill on your behalf. If you attempt to smother too late you may take the full force of the kick.

3) CATCH THE KICKING LEG:

Edge carefully forward toward the kicker, all the time looking for the opportunity to grab him. When he kicks, catch his kicking leg with your lead hand, (left hand if in orthodox stance, right hand if in southpaw stance) either under the ankle or by the trouser leg. Grab his attire (jacket, shirt etc.) with your right hand and pull him into grappling range. Any grappling attack may be executed from here, though the opponent, now stood on one leg is open for a major inner-reaping throw.

4) SIDE STEP: (and parry)

Edge carefully forward forcing the opponent to retreat or kick. When he does kick move your right, back leg across and behind to your left, side stepping the kick. For extra safety you may add a small parry at this point to block the kick, redirecting it away form you. As the kick is about to connect with your body strike the outside of the attacker's shin (inside of the shin if the opponent is kicking with his left foot) with the inside of your right wrist, by striking in a downward and right lateral (your right) motion simultaneously with the side step. As soon as the opponent's kicking leg lands on the floor (or even as it is about to land) grab and pull him in to grappling range. If his attack is right footed he will land with his back to you, ideally positioned for the aforementioned 'rear chokes' (Chapter 4 - Reverse Naked Choke).

Alternatively, you may parry the opponent's kicking leg in the opposite direction, striking the leg with the outside wrist of your leading arm in a downward left lateral (your left) motion, striking the inside of the attacker's shin (outside of the shin if the opponent attacks with his left foot) whilst simultaneously moving your back right leg across and behind to your right. If you block the opponent's right leg he will land facing toward you, if you block his left leg he will land facing away from you, again primed for the reverse naked choke hold.

6) ON RETRACTION OF THE KICKING LEG:

By far the safest and best bet, the skill factor is also relatively low. As ever, edge carefully toward the opponent, take any opportunity offered to 'grab and pull'. If none arises wait for the opponent to kick, when he does, step just outside of the kick's range by sliding your rear, right foot backwards. As the kick is being retracted rush forward and grab the opponent, pulling him in to grappling range, or alternatively push him over whilst his balance is impaired. For best effect 'grab' or 'push' before the opponent replaces his kicking leg back on the ground.

7) ABSORB THE KICK AND GRAB:

This principle is not so 'kamakazi' as it may sound, though it can be a little risky. Edge carefully forward toward the opponent, always looking out for the chance to 'grab and pull', if none arises wait for the opponent to kick. It is important here to show the opponent no vital targets such as your groin or lower abdomen, keep your body angled and your guard tightly protecting your ribs and chin, forcing the opponent to kick a non vulnerable target. The instant the kick lands take the force of the blow on your guard, grab and pull him in to grappling range before he can recover his kicking leg. Alternatively, push him over whilst his kicking leg is still off the ground.

8) THE RUSH:

A very simple strategy with a low skill factor. Utilized (usually inadvertently) by street fighters all the time. As soon as you face the kicker, or at any time during the altercation 'rush in', impervious to any attack the opponent may employ, and grab/pull him in to grappling range, if he employs a kick as you 'rush' you may push him over. The obvious danger here is getting kicked as you move in, which, in theory, may seem likely. In reality, against the street fighter it is not so likely.

The quicker you can 'bridge the gap' the better this strategy works.

Though the forgoing strategies cover most scenarios you may find defences and 'gap bridging' strategies of your own invention, as long as they fall in to the realms of effectiveness, use them. From my experience the grappler often has to 'take' a few shots before he can 'bridge the gap', once he does bridge it he very rarely loses.

Chapter Ten

Beating The Puncher

It is a far more dangerous animal you face when you front the 'puncher', though he is often heavily shackled by his slavery to distancing, he needs to be close to employ punching technique, so close that you can often reach out and pull him in to grappling range.

As with Chapter 9 - Beating the Kicker, we are not dealing here with the advanced or elite player, more the novice puncher who missiles wild swings or uncontrolled lunging punches. The defence strategies employed against this genre of fighter come mostly in the form of 'ducks' and 'slips'.

The puncher should be treated in the same way as the kicker, with perhaps a little more caution, break down his distance and 'grab'. He will of course have less of a gap to bridge than the kicker though the likelihood of being 'stopped' en route by a puncher is higher than that of the kicker, so as always care should be taken.

All of the time whilst facing the puncher you should edge carefully forward, killing his distance, forcing him to retreat or punch. A retreating novice puncher is a beaten man, it takes a skilled pugilist to punch whilst in reverse. If you stand off and give the puncher the distance he craves, you are, in effect, giving him the fight. The puncher is at his strongest against a stationary or retreating opponent. Always try to keep the puncher moving backwards.

Here are my chosen strategies against the puncher.

Once the gap is closed and a hold secured on the opponent you may attack with any of the techniques described in the latter chapters. As you carefully move towards the opponent keep your head moving (bob and weave) side to side, up and down, a moving target is harder to hit.

1) DUCK
2) SLIP
3) LAY BACK
4) STEP BACK
5) GUARD BLOCK
6) RUSH

All of the forthcoming defences/close downs should be employed from a 45 degree, compact left or right lead front stance. Once a hold is secured up on the adversary employ appropriate techniques, as detailed in foregoing chapters.

1) DUCK:

Edge carefully toward the puncher, forcing him to retreat or punch. If the opportunity arises grab and pull the opponent in to grappling range. If not, wait for him to throw a punch, when he does, duck underneath the punch by bending at the knees, (as opposed to the waist) as the punch goes over your head grab and pull the opponent into grappling range.

2) THE SLIP:

The slip is best used against straight line punches (as opposed to hooks or uppercuts). Edge carefully towards the puncher, forcing him to retreat or punch. If the opportunity arises grab and pull the opponent in to grappling range. If not, wait for him to punch. When he does, slip inside or outside the punch so that it goes past the side of your head, as it does so grab and pull the opponent in to grappling range. This defence/close down is often used inadvertently by participants in street scenarios, however, the skill factor when trying to do the same thing deliberately is very high.

3) LAY BACK:

Edge carefully toward the puncher, forcing him to retreat or punch. If the opportunity arises grab and pull the opponent in to grappling range. If not, wait for him to punch. When he does lay back out side the punch's range by transferring the weight from your leading leg (right or left according to which is leading) to your back leg, bending it just enough to take you out side of the punch's range. As the attacker is retracting the punch lunge forward, by transferring the weight back on to the front leg, grab and pull the opponent in to grappling range.

4) STEP BACK:

The step back is almost a direct facsimile to the lay back. As the attacking punch comes toward your head step back (as opposed to lay back) with your rear leg, just enough to take you out of the punch's range. As the attacker retracts his punch lunge forward, grab and pull him in to grappling range.

5) GUARD BLOCK:

The strategy with the guard block is to edge forward carefully, forcing the opponent to retreat or punch. Be sure to engage a tight guard, elbows protecting your ribs, fists protecting your jaw, at all times. When the attacker punches takes the force of the blow/s on your guard, when you get close enough grab and pull him in to grappling range, preferably when the opponent is retracting his punch.

6) RUSH:

Ignore all safety aspects formerly recommended and RUSH the opponent, this may be done at any time in the proceedings, try to ignore anything that the opponent may throw at you, just get close and grab, pulling him in to grappling range.

BEWARE!! Though it is not probable it is possible that you may get hurt using this kind of manoeuvre.

Real Grappling

All of the foregoing may be practised safely in the controlled environment of the dojo/gym with a willing partner. Initially practise the close downs with little or no resistance from your partner. When competence and confidence is gained increase the intensity of the opponent's attack and resistance until you are able to 'go' all out.

It is important not to just concentrate on bridging the gap, once the gap has been effectively bridged you should practise the techniques you wish to employ once 'inside'.

Chapter Eleven

Beating The Street Fighter

What is a street fighter? This is what we need to determine before we set about dealing with his downfall.

Firstly I would say that the street fighter is the only genre of fighter I fear more as an adversary than the grappler. Why? Because he is a grappler, kicker, puncher and all round dirty fighter who will stop at nothing, employing anything and everything in his quest to win. He will dish out pain mercilessly and 'take it' just as readily. He will, can and does strike at any time, usually when you least expect it, when you're blinking, coughing, drinking, lifting a cigarette to your mouth, eating, even when your kissing your girlfriend, nothing is sacred with this veritable fighting chameleon.

If you have a weakness he will engineer it until it is a gaping hole that he'll walk right through, if you have a particular strength he will force you to fight with it to your blind side. As far as I can see, and from my experience, the street fighter has only one weakness, his fitness. Usually the street fighter is a 'natural', some one that hasn't had to train to acquire his ability, due to this hereditary fighting prowess he doesn't train as much as he should leaving him vulnerable in the one area that does not often effect him because he is so used to 'finishing it' quickly. Anyone who takes him beyond a minute has a good chance of winning.

Before you get too distressed I should state that 'good' street fighters are a rarity, of the thousands I know and the hundreds I have fought, who all see themselves as 'street fighters', there are only three or four who I personally would class as 'good' (though all of them would, no doubt, class themselves as good). So do not despair, the good ones are rarer than a poll tax rebate (which is a very rare animal indeed).

Here lies the problem, the dilemma, the complication. How do you know, on face value, who is and is not 'good'? How do you differentiate between the two? You don't. And neither does it matter, because when violence is about to be force fed you, to wonder is to hesitate and hesitation begets defeat. If I may be so bold as to quote directly from my first book **Watch my Back - A Bouncer's Story**, (NO PLUG INTENDED, HONESTLY!)

*"What helps the street fighter swim clear from the maelstrom of trained fighters is that he lacks very little. Every technique has been tried and tested in the 'live' scenario, nothing is left to theory. He can kick, punch and grapple like he was born to do it. Most trained fighters are still embryos in the womb of combat while the street fighter is fully matured. He controls the 'duck syndrome' (a technique used to veil fear) with expertise and puts most people out of a fight before they even know that they are in it. He is a fighting chameleon, adapting himself to any given situation and changing his fight plan accordingly. When faced with an opponent who is, or appears to be, a bit 'handy' he may act weak or scared so as to mentally disarm them, then strike out fiercely when least expected to. If the opponent looks as though he may have a 'chink' in his mental armour the street fighter may act over confident or strong to psyche him out and back him down, thus winning without 'casting a blow', or if and when necessary a combination of the both (See **Real Self Defence** 'adrenalin switches').*

When the fighting has commenced the street fighter will, if he hasn't already finished the fight, assess the opponent's artillery automatically and fight them at their weakest range, forcing a kicker to punch or a puncher to kick or a puncher/kicker to grapple etc."

Everybody that fights on the street sees himself as a street fighter, though in reality most of them are just useless brawlers, lacking in style, speed, knowledge or bottle (some times all at once) fighting only from the podium of an alcohol/drug induced bravery.

There are 'talkers' who can 'talk the talk'. These cover 95 per cent of street fighters, they talk a good fight and have more 'front' than Woolworths, but that's about their limit. Then there is the latter 5 per cent, the 'walkers', (no, not the crisps) who really can 'walk the walk', with these babies you are going to have to fight for your very life. To segregate the talkers from the walkers you have to take them right up to the doorway of violence, the walkers will open the door, the talkers will balk.

The greatest asset to take with you into a confrontation with a street fighter is 'savvy' (common sense). Look out for all the dirty tricks, the distractions that will leave you momentarily vulnerable, long enough for the street fighter to take away your consciousness. These distractions usually come in the guise of 'line ups', where your adversary will 'talk' as a distracting tool, even telling you that he doesn't want to fight before he hits you. If you are vigilant you will easily spot the 'line up', the assailant will move his feet for better positioning, splay his arms as though exclaiming, his aggressiveness will increase or, if he is employing the disarming approach he will feign supplication, he'll probably move closer to you and become very tactile to insure a 'good shot'. If you can actually get past this stage with out 'catching one' you're in with a good chance.

In grappling range most street fighters love to bite, butt and gouge, some have a basic knowledge of chokes. Few hold the full range of grappling techniques (unless they have read this book too) at their disposal. What they do have in bagfuls, which seems to compensate for their lack of technique, is determination and guts, they won't give in, you'll have to really hurt them to stop them.

When facing this genre of fighter leave your morals in the safe hands of your second, to take them into battle against the street fighter is to heavily shackle yourself with unwanted and unrealistic restrictions, Morals will surely help you lose. I have witnessed the decimated remains of many a fighter being dragged from the claws of a street fight saying to his friends and seconds, disbelievingly, "He bit me!!" As though it wasn't allowed.

When faced by one (or several) of life's gratuitously violent minority don't be naive, anything goes. Don't try to be a gentleman, it is only seen as a weakness, if you want to survive against these people you have to be as bad or worse than them, at least for the time it takes to neutralise them.

Here are a few suggested defences to utilise whilst in grappling range against the street fighter.

For defences against Punching and Kicking please refer to the chapters on the same.

BITES:
If the adversary tries to bite your face (ears etc) move your head away from his teeth and then rapidly butt him. The quicker your are able to secure a head or neck lock on him the better, once he is 'locked' he can no longer bite.

EYE GOUGE:
Thrash your head away form the attacker's fingers, if possible bite the fingers or twist them into finger locks.

HEAD BUTT:

Keep your chin tightly in to your chest, this will protect your jaw and face from 'butting'. If he butts you above the eye line he will hurt himself as much as you.

The biggest question here is whether your bottle can outlast the street fighter's stamina, if it can you will win.

As a final point on the street fighter, beware of the plea bargaining adversary who will offer the earth to be freed from a lock or hold that you may have up on him, when you release the hold they attack again with added ferocity. Whether or not you do let the 'plea bargainor' out of your hold is your prerogative, if you do beware of the aforementioned 'con'.

Chapter Twelve

Inanimate Objects

Inanimate objects can be a great aid to the grappler. Doors, tables, walls etc. can aid leverage and act as battering rams to smash or throw an opponent into. Again, whether or not you wish to employ the theories with in this chapter is your prerogative. Some may see the inclusion of 'inanimate objects' in a book of this genre as 'barbaric'. Personally I see all violence as barbaric, whether you push an adversary's head into the corner of an open door or knock him out with a neck lock you are inflicting pain up on another human being, neither is justifiable, both are perversely wrong, but, if survival is your aim, and I'm presuming that it is, then that's the shade of light that you have to live under.

Often within the violent midst of an altercation you find your self in the most precarious of positions, under tables, in doorways, tangled around bus shelters, even in large, circular, concrete dust bins (see **Watch my back - A Bouncer's Story** for an in-depth on the embarrassing episode which saw me fighting in/from a concrete dustbin, Oh the embarrassment) etc. etc. There are hundreds of different scenarios that offer inanimate objects as a crutch, those that follow are 'appetisers', the seed that, hopefully will flower many more.

DOORS:
A door may be used to 'slam' on the head of an adversary who falls between 'door' and 'frame'. You may 'slam' an opponent's back into the edge of an open door or the door handle, throw him in to the edge of an open door or push his head in to the handle or edge of an open door.

WALLS:
Ideal for pushing an opponent's head into, throwing him into or choking him against.

LEDGES:
(This includes 'sills', curbs, table/chair edges or any other objects with a ledge or curb). Ideal; for slamming heads, backs or limbs against, throwing an opponent against etc.

MOVEABLES:
Any thing moveable may be pulled onto a horizontal opponent (if it is heavy) or picked up and used as an incidental weapon.

BROOMSTICK/BRUSH:
The stalk of a brush may be used to strike or choke an adversary (they're not bad for 'sweeps' either).

PEN/PENCIL:
May be probed in to the sensitive areas of the opponent's body (or used to write him a very nasty letter).

The list is, potentially endless so I shall not bore you with more, as you can clearly see everything and anything can and may be used as an aid to repel an adversary, some I dare not mention for reasons of a legal nature, it is enough to restate that every thing is a potential incidental defensive weapon, and to not recognise this is to leave out a small though imperative fracture of the multifarious 'grappling jigsaw'.

Chapter Thirteen

Training Equipment

Working with the live partner is without doubt the best method of practising grappling movements (Dead ones just don't react the same) though other methods may add to this practise.

PUNCH BAG:

Not traditionally known as a grappler's training implement due to its pugilistic heritage, though it can be a great aid to the practise of horizontal grappling.

All of the strikes prescribed in Chapter 5 - Horizontal Grappling, can be practised on the bag effectively. Encase the bag in a sack or old clothes and realism for vertical grappling is greatly heightened enabling you to 'grab', 'pull' and 'strike'. With the aid of the 'clothed bag' the footwork section of many throws may also be practised effectively. A six foot, heavy bag (dressed) may be stood on the floor and used for all aspects of vertical grappling, including most throws.

KARATE/JUDO BELT:

The belt may be hooked around a sturdy object at shoulder level (wall bars, heavy swing frame etc.) and used for practising throw footwork by gripping the belt ends in either hand about midway up the belt, as though gripping an opponent's attire, and pulling on the belt as you practise the appropriate footwork.

SHADOW SPARRING:

This is an excellent method of practising throw and strike footwork. Draw or form a cross on the floor, stand so that your left foot and right foot are in opposite squares and place an imaginary opponent directly opposite you. Place your hands in an imagined grip and practise the footwork to any chosen throw, strike or combination. Use the lines on the cross to check correct foot positioning.

BENCH PRESS: (CHEST)

Lie flat on a the bench, grip the bar bell (with the desired weight attached) at a comfortable width, (no less than shoulder width) lower the weight down until the bar touches your chest, inhale as the bar is lowered, push the weight back to the start position, exhaling as you push the bar back. Repeat this movement for ten repetitions, then rest. After a reasonable recuperation time repeat for a further ten reps, rest, and then a final set of ten reps.

MILITARY PRESS: (SHOULDERS)

Sitting on a bench (or standing up) lift the bar bell to your chest with an inverted grip, from here push the bar above your head until your arms lock straight, exhaling, then lower the bar back to your chest, inhaling. Repeat the overhead push element of the movement for ten reps, Rest, ten more reps, rest and then a final ten reps.

BENT OVER ROWING: (BACK MUSCLES)

From a standing position bend from the waist so that your torso is at a right angle with your legs, pick the weighted bar bell from the floor (inverted grip), maintaining the right angle with back and legs. Pull the weight up until the bar touches your chest, exhaling, then lower the bar back to arms length, inhaling. Repeat for ten reps. Three set with a short rest in between each.

SQUATS: (LEGS)

Resting the bar bell, evenly balanced across the back of your shoulders, hold firmly by the bar from the back with both hands at about shoulder width. Stand with feet shoulder width apart and squat down to the floor by bending your legs, keep your back straight, head up. Inhaling on decent. Push back up to your original start position, exhaling as you rise, repeat for ten reps, three sets with a rest in between each.

CURLS: (FRONT UPPER ARM)

Pick the weighted bar bell (or dumb bells) up with a reverse grip, (palms facing away from your body) arms straight. Curl the bar up until it touches your chest, exhaling, then lower it back to the original start position, inhaling. Repeat for ten reps, three sets with a rest in between each.

TRICEP EXTENSION: (BACK UPPER ARM)

Lying, back on the bench with the weighted bar at arms length, close grip (less than shoulder width) above your chest with your palms facing to your feet. Lower the weight, with out moving your elbows, until the bar touches your forehead, inhaling, then straighten your arms back to the original start position, exhaling. Repeat for ten reps, three sets with a short rest in between each.

All of the forgoing should, for safety reasons, be practised with the aid of a partner or 'spot' who may relieve you of the weight should you 'fail' a repetition, or there is a danger of you dropping the weight and injuring yourself.

Chapter Fourteen

Extra Curriculum

Good grappling requires a lot of skill, this is acquired through the regular practise of the grappling movements in a controlled environment. Stamina and strength are two other necessaries which are also developed in the conscientious practise of controlled grappling, if you can increase your stamina and strength levels with extra curriculum training (which you definitely can) it goes without saying that everything else about your grappling work will improve.

RUNNING:
A great cardiovascular exercise that will build the stamina ever needed by the grappler, lack of stamina will relegate even the highly skilled to lacklustre.

Long endurance runs (2 miles plus) are more recommended than short sprints, the latter is better suited to the disciplines that demand short bursts of energy (power and Olympic weight lifting etc.) The grappler must build and expand his lung capacity to prepare for long, gruelling fights. Adding a hundred yard sprint midway through the long run or at the end can be a great attribute to stamina building.

Three times a week (more if you wish) will suffice. In a relatively short space of time your stamina levels will increase markedly. Do not worry if, initially, you struggle, mentally and/or physically, with this extra curriculum exercise, in time it gets easier, even enjoyable. When a routine has been established running is/can be a very therapeutic exercise, I see no other fitness exercise to better it.

WEIGHT TRAINING:

A much misunderstood method of physical training. In days of old it was thought that working out with weights made you muscular but stiff and immobile. Of course in these days of great enlightenment we recognise this to be untrue (the stiff and immobile bit) and identify weight training for what it really is, a first class method of developing the body and an excellent aid, not only to the grappler but any sportsman with a hunger for success.

I can think of no better strength building exercise than weight training, a huge amount of brute strength is needed in the execution of many of the grappling movements, especially in ground work. Weight training is first class preparation.

How much emphasis you, as an individual, place up on the practise of weights is entirely up to you, if you intend to take it up seriously then a qualified instructor at an appropriate gym will show you the correct method of practice and advise you on the best diet for your needs. It is out of this book's context to enlarge on the subject.

The following exercises will though give you a basic start.
Before handling weights be sure to warm up, stretching and suppling the muscles.

When beginning weight training concentrate on the major muscle groups, chest, back, shoulders, arms and legs, working the said muscle groups with fundamental exercises.

The amount of weight to use on the different exercises will depend entirely upon the strength of the individual practising. Suffice it to say that you should get (initially) 10 comfortable repetitions with the weight that you are using.

Epilogue

As you will have surmised from the latter text, grappling is a many splendoured art, effective in the highest extreme. But, as formerly stated, it is largely ignored by most combative systems who see not its importance. Paradoxically, those who do adhere to the grappling arts seem to do so at the cost of everything else, using their grappling techniques as a first line attack and neglecting other combative ranges, (punching, kicking) which in my opinion makes them as blinkered and naive as their pugilistic and kick orientated brothers in arms.

Combat is a metaphoric jigsaw that is not complete with out all of the former pieces. A complete combat system should incorporate all distances, theories and tactics instead of hiding behind the smoke screen of mysticism and "my system is the best, I don't need anything else." We, all of us, need 'something else', we all need to beg, steal or borrow from other systems. The Martial arts should bring its exponents enlightenment, enlightenment in layman's terms is 'removing the blinkers' so that full combat perspective can be observed (and in fact life's full perspective).

Anyone who has 'found their way' and observed full perspective will, I'm sure, agree with the Kick, punch, grapple theory. Each range is strongly independent and yet incomplete in its sovereignty, amalgamation of the three is pivotal if practicality is to be sought.

Although this book centres upon grappling it should be seen as a 'support' book. Grappling? A 'support' art? I do believe the grappler to be potentate amongst fighters on a 'one on one' basis, unfortunately the street scenario is a far cry from 'one on one', nine times out of ten you will be faced with several adversaries and to tie your hands up by courting grappling as a first line attack is foolhardy and dangerous, grappling techniques should be employed as a last resort, to back up a failed punch (your own punch) or to combat a 'blind side' grab. Even the 'one on one' situation deems you vulnerable to friends of your grappling adversary who will kick/punch or even stab you as you fight for a hold on their compatriot (believe me, I've been there).

Grappling is a wonderfully intricate, effective fighting art which should be given equal practise time with punching/kicking. In the live scenario it should be employed as a last resort.

All of the techniques prescribed herein should be worked to second nature status, it is never enough to look at the pictures and expect the moves to work for you, there is no substitute for hard work.